SHRUBS

SHRUBS

Grange
BOOKS

A QUANTUM BOOK

Published by Grange Books
an imprint of Grange Books Plc
The Grange
Kingsnorth Industrial Estate
Hoo, nr. Rochester
Kent ME3 9ND

ISBN 1-84013-269-8

This book is produced by
Quantum Books Ltd
6 Blundell Street
London N7 9BH

Project Manager: Rebecca Kingsley
Project Editor: Judith Millidge
Design/Editorial: David Manson
Andy McColm, Maggie Manson

The material in this publication previously appeared in
Flowering Trees and Shrubs

QUMSPSH
Set in Futura
Reproduced in Singapore by Eray Scan
Printed in Singapore by Star Standard Industries (Pte) Ltd

Contents

SUPERB SHRUBS

There are few plants that have the versatility of shrubs. They provide a garden with a sense of shape, texture and colour throughout the year. They can be used purely for their decorative effect, or as boundary hedging or screening for unsightly objects and areas. Not only will they be decorative in their own right, but they will also form a background against which other plants may be displayed at their best.

Shrub Selection

Shrubs often become permanent residents in a garden; unlike many herbaceous plants they tend to live for a long time. It may even be many years before the plant has sufficiently established itself to come into flower.

PRE-PLANNED SITING

Both their longevity and the time they take to mature into flower, plus the great difficulty of moving such large plants once they have become established, means that great care and forethought must be exercised over the siting and planting of new shrubs.

CAREFUL SELECTION

Another general point to bear in mind is that shrubs can grow into very large plants, not only in their height and girth but also in their underground parts, which can develop into an extensive network of hungry and thirsty roots. Care is required when selecting shrubs.

Left. Berberis darwinii – *an evergreen shrub with bright golden yellow flowers.*

Above. Magnolia stellata *resents any form of disturbance once it is planted.*

GENERAL LAYOUT

Garden design is very much a personal matter. However, it is not something done very frequently by most people and so advice can be helpful. The choice of plants and general atmosphere of the garden is a matter of personal taste. In the same way that the design of the interior of a house reflects the taste of the occupants. You are the one who has to live with your garden, and like it, and so the general layout is crucial.

The choice of colours; the balance between flowers and greenery, and between lawn and borders or other features; all should be in tune with your taste and lifestyle. In a sense, shrubs can be likened to the exterior fabric of the house, once established, they are very permanent, without going through a major upheaval. The message for anyone designing a garden is to keep it simple, particularly in the small garden where it is very important to avoid overplanting.

Effective Shrub Siting

Even in a comparatively small garden, shrubs can be used to provide a sense of drama and adventure by obscuring sections of the garden, which suddenly come into view as a corner is turned.

SHRUBS IN WINTER

Winter flowering shrubs can be ugly during the summer, so they should not be planted in too much of a prominent position. On the other hand, they should ideally be placed where they can be seen from the house or from a path as in the winter you don't want to have to walk far to see them.

SHRUBBERIES

Shrubberies are now considered old-fashioned and except in large gardens, it is rare to see borders devoted purely to shrubs. But with careful selection, a shrubbery can provide a relatively trouble-free, yet very attractive addition to any garden, offering as it does, colour throughout most of the year.

Left. Fuschias such as 'Mrs Popple' can be trimmed back each year giving them a natural affinity with herbaceous borders.

Above. Wisteria floribunda can climb over any structure including walls of houses, fences or trellises.

MIXED BORDERS

More common than shrubberies, mixed borders, just as their name suggests are a mixture of different plants: shrubs, herbaceous and even annual and bedding plants. Although, herbaceous borders, strictly speaking, should be restricted to herbaceous plants, some shrubs such as fuchsias and buddleias are cut to the ground each year and so are treated as herbaceous plants. They provide a more permanent framework and offer shade to smaller plants.

WALL AND FENCES

Walls are often clothed with shrubs and climbers for several reasons. A wall or fence may afford admirable protection to some tender shrubs during the winter, and it can be a good foil to set off the flowers or foliage of the plants. Walls and fences add a vertical element to a garden, they act as solid supports for climbing plants and conversely they are sometimes ugly. New fences in particular often need plants to hide or soften them.

11

Shrub Environment

As well as the details that we have already discussed, there are two other very important factors which need to be taken into account when deciding which shrubs to choose and where they should be positioned in the garden : the soil and the weather.

SOIL CONDITIONS

Soil can vary in both its chemistry and its structure. Most shrubs will grow in neutral or acid soils as long as the latter is not too acidic. Alkaline or chalky soils present more of a problem. Some plants such as rhododendrons or pierises will not tolerate any alkalinity and will even regress when irrigated with hard chalky water.

If you live on chalky soil you may have to avoid some plants or grow the smaller species in pots or beds of neutral or acidic soil. Soil-testing kits can be bought very cheaply and will allow you to discover which type of soil you have. These kits indicate the pH level of the soil: pH7 shows you have neutral soil, above pH7 is alkaline, below pH7 is acidic.

Left. Rhododendrons – many people are denied the chance to grow these shrubs because of their hatred of chalky soil.

Above. Choisya ternata is not at all fussy about soils or about siting, but it will flower better in full sun.

WEATHER CONDITIONS

There are three aspects of the weather to take into account: sun, wind and frost. Look carefully at the entries in the directory section later in this book (see p.16) before siting a shrub, because some will only grow in full sun, while others prefer shady conditions. Many plants will tolerate either sun or shade, but generally they will not flower well in shade. They might also get drawn; their shape being weedy and out of character.

Windy sites should be given some form of protection. Ornamental shrubs can be severely damaged by strong winds, and shelter belts of wind-resistant trees or shrubs should be planted as soon as possible. Hardiness to frost should also be borne in mind. Each plant in the directory section has been given an indication of hardiness. Susceptible, tender shrubs should be sited in warmer parts of the garden, particularly against sunny walls or fences.

Cultivation of Shrubs

Before any shrub can be planted, the site should be thoroughly prepared. The gardener wants every one of his progeny to succeed. Site preparation is one of the ways to help ensure they are given the best chance.

PREPARING THE GROUND

All perennial weeds should be completely cleared away; there is nothing worse than trying to remove persistent weeds from established shrubs particularly if the latter are multiple stemmed or suckered. Beds should be well-dug with plenty of organic material added. Serious consideration should also be given to drainage.

PLANTING

Shrubs that have been purchased bare-rooted may be planted between autumn and the spring, providing the ground is not frozen. Container-grown plants can be planted at any time, providing the ground is not frozen or baked hard. Container plants should be watered an hour or so before planting and roots teased out.

Left. Mahonia japonica *is able to bring dark corners of the garden alive in winter, when its beautiful flowers stand out.*

Above. Removal of old wood on shrubs such as the Buddleia *will help generate stronger growth in the spring.*

AFTERCARE

The ground around the shrub should be kept free of weeds until the plant is established. Mulching with organic material such as wood bark or laying black plastic over the ground will not only keep the weeds down but will also help preserve water. Water is crucial to a newly planted tree and the ground should not be allowed to go short of moisture. Bonemeal or a general fertiliser can be applied in early spring to feed the plant.

PRUNING

This can be a worrying topic for many gardeners. They are never certain when to prune and how much to remove; consequently shrubs are often neglected and too little is cut off. When in doubt it is probably safer to err on the side of underpruning. All shrubs should have dead or damaged wood pruned away. This will help to promote new growth and can also encourage the rejuvenation of the plant and the flowers.

SHRUB SPECIES

Key to symbols

The following icons are used throughout this directory to help provide a snapshot of the idiosyncrasies of each species.

Height (m) or (cm) **2 m**

BLOOMING PERIOD

Spring PERIOD **1**   PERIOD **2** Summer

Autumn PERIOD **3**   PERIOD **4** Winter

HARDINESS

Hardy   Semi-hardy   Tender

LEAF TYPES

Evergreen   Semi-evergreen

Deciduous

ABELIA x GRANDIFLORA COPPER GLOW

This shrub is sometimes called 'Glossy Abelia' because of its shiny leaves. It is one of the best of the abelias, with large pink and white, slightly fragrant tubular flowers appearing over a long period from mid-summer until autumn.

Common name Copper Glow.
Height 2m (6ft).
Colour Pink and white flowers.
Flowering time Mid Summer.
Hardiness Hardy.
Leaves Semi-evergreen.

2 m — PERIOD 2

ACACIA ARMATA KANGAROO THORN

This shrub is also known as Kangaroo Thorn. It has small finely cut leaves and thorny spines on the stems. Its main attraction is the mass of bright yellow flowers in spring. In colder areas, it is best grown as a conservatory or greenhouse plant.

Common name Kangaroo Thorn.
Height 3m (10ft).
Colour Bright yellow flowers.
Flowering time Spring.
Hardiness Tender.
Leaves Semi-evergreen.

3 m — PERIOD 1

BERBERIS DARWINII CHILEAN BARBERRY

This is a popular evergreen species with small, toothed, shiny green leaves. In spring it is covered in masses of hanging panicles of golden-yellow flowers and in autumn with blue-black fruit. Forms a dense shrub good for hedging along a north border.

Common name Chilean Barberry.
Height 2m (6ft).
Colour Golden-yellow flowers.
Flowering time Spring.
Hardiness Hardy.
Leaves Evergreen.

BERBERIS x STENOPHYLLA BARBERRY

This is a dense shrub with long arching stems covered with golden-yellow flowers in spring. This berberis has a good strong scent with narrow leaves, silvery on the underside. This species can be overpowering in all but the largest borders, but makes an excellent specimen plant.

Common name Barberry.
Height 3m (10ft).
Colour Golden-yellow flowers.
Flowering time Spring.
Hardiness Hardy.
Leaves Semi-evergreen.

BUDDLEIA ALTERNIFOLIA BUTTERFLY BUSH

This shrub has arching branches with clusters of fragrant lilac flowers. It is one of the hardiest species and will form a small tree suitable for planting in a lawn. Pruning should be confined to removing some of the old wood after flowering.

Common name Butterfly Bush.
Height 3m (10ft).
Colour Lilac flowers.
Flowering time Summer, autumn.
Hardiness Hardy.
Leaves Deciduous.

3
m

PERIOD
2-3

BUDDLEIA FALLOWIANA LOCH INCH

This shrub has very fragrant lavender flowers on white woolly stems. This is a tender shrub and should be given a sheltered position. There is a white form, 'Alba'.

Common name Loch Inch.
Height 3m (10ft).
Colour Lavender flowers.
Flowering time Summer, autumn.
Hardiness Tender.
Leaves Deciduous.

3
m

PERIOD
2-3

CALLUNA VULGARIS 'DARKNESS' HEATHER

This is a lime-hating plant and cannot be grown on alkaline soils. Full sun is preferred but they will tolerate a little shade. A good ground cover plant, useful for filling between plants, especially in front of conifers.

Common name Heather.
Height 30cm (1ft).
Colour Pink-purple flowers.
Flowering time Autumn.
Hardiness Hardy.
Leaves Evergreen.

 30 cm **PERIOD 3**

CAMELLIA JAPONICA 'ADOLPHE AUDUSSON' CAMELLIA

This is one of the most popular, with its blood-red, semi-double flowers. Best planted in an acid, peaty soil as they are unhappy in alkaline conditions. Plant in a site where they will be sheltered from cold winds and the early-morning sun, as sudden variation in conditions can destroy flower buds.

Common name Camellia.
Height 3m (10ft).
Colour Blood-red flowers.
Flowering time Spring.
Hardiness Semi-hardy.
Leaves Evergreen.

 3 m **PERIOD 1**

CALLUNA/CAMELLIA

CEANOTHUS ARBOREUS CALIFORNIAN LILAC

One of the more vigorous of the evergreens, with sky blue, scented flowers. The flowers are very small, but since they appear in large clusters that cover the whole bush, they give an impression of a mass of blue with little green visible. They dislike pure chalk and need the protection of a wall in colder areas.

Common name Californian Lilac.
Height 4m (13ft).
Colour Sky blue, scented flowers.
Flowering time Summer.
Hardiness Tender.
Leaves Evergreen.

 4 m PERIOD 2

CHAENOMELES JAPONICA ORNAMENTAL QUINCE

This is a very hardy shrub that produces masses of waxy flowers, resembling apple blossoms in shape. These are tightly clustered to the bare branches before the leaves the emerge. They can be used as a free-standing shrub, but will happily grow on a north wall.

Common name Ornamental Quince.
Height 3m (10ft).
Colour Red, pink or white flowers.
Flowering time Spring.
Hardiness Hardy.
Leaves Semi-evergreen.

 3 m PERIOD 1

CHOISYA TERNATA MEXICAN ORANGE

A popular shrub with waxy, white
flowers which are highly scented. If the
summer weather is hot and sunny,
another flush of flowers will appear in
autumn. This shrub is not fussy about
siting but will flower better in full sun.

Common name Mexican Orange.
Height 2m (6ft).
Colour Creamy white flowers.
Flowering time Spring, summer.
Hardiness Hardy.
Leaves Evergreen.

 2 m PERIOD 1-2

CISTUS LADNIFER ROCK ROSE

One of the most popular of the cistus
species having white flowers with a
deep red blotch at the base of the
petals. The flowers are rose-shaped
and short lasting. Most species are salt
tolerant and make good seaside plants.

Common name Rock Rose.
Height 3m (10ft).
Colour White flowers.
Flowering time Summer.
Hardiness Semi-hardy.
Leaves Deciduous.

 3 m PERIOD 2

CLEMATIS

CLEMATIS 'NELLY MOSER' CLEMATIS

A favourite climber whose flowers are a
pale mauvy-pink, 23cm (9in) across,
with a a darker stripe running down the
centre of the petal. Need shade at the
base to keep the roots cool. Wilt is a
common problem in initial stages, but
the plant will normally produce growth
again the next year.

Common name Clematis.
Height 3m (10ft).
Colour Pale mauvy-pink flowers.
Flowering time Spring.
Hardiness Hardy.
Leaves Deciduous.

CLEMATIS JACKMANII CLEMATIS

The flowers of this species are purple
and are 15cm (6in) across and it is one
of the most popular clematis. It has a
form 'Superba' with even richer colour
and fuller petals.

Common name Clematis.
Height 3m (10ft).
Colour Purple flowers.
Flowering time Summer.
Hardiness Hardy.
Leaves Deciduous.

CORNUS ALBA RED-BARKED DOGWOOD

C. alba is a bushy, vigorous Asiatic
shrub. It is extremely decorative with
bright red bark which looks wonderful
in winter and attractive foliage and
flowers the rest of the year.

Common name Red-barked
Dogwood.
Height 3m (10ft).
Colour Pale mauvy-pink flowers.
Flowering time Spring.
Hardiness Hardy.
Leaves Deciduous.

3 m | PERIOD 1

CORNUS CANADENSIS DOGWOOD

A very low growing shrub that makes
it an excellent ground-cover, particularly
in shady positions. The flower itself is
insignificant but sits as a central boss in
four white bracts, giving the impression
of a much bigger flower. Useful to
brighten up the area under trees.

Common name Dogwood.
Height 20cm (8in).
Colour White flowers.
Flowering time Spring, summer.
Hardiness Hardy.
Leaves Deciduous.

20 cm | PERIOD 1-2

COTINUS COGGYRIA 'ROYAL PURPLE' SMOKE BUSH

Extremely attractive both in leaf and flower, this shrub is a good all-round specimen. They prefer full sun, but can tolerate light shade. The leaves are a very dark purple, emphasised with the sun setting behind it. The flowers are silken threads on loose panicles, giving the impression of smoke.

Common name Smoke Bush.
Height 2m (6ft).
Colour Pale pink flowers.
Flowering time Summer.
Hardiness Hardy.
Leaves Deciduous.

2 m

PERIOD 2

CYTISUS SCOPARIUS BROOM

In spring this shrub produces a splash of colour with its thousands of pea-like flowers. The flowers are carried on long, thin arching stems. Position in a sunny spot but not in limy soils. A short-lived plant useful as a temporary planting in between other slower growing shrubs.

Common name Broom.
Height 3m (10ft).
Colour Yellow flowers.
Flowering time Spring.
Hardiness Hardy.
Leaves Deciduous.

3 m

PERIOD 1

DEUTZIA x MAGNIFICA DEUTZIA

This is an erect shrub with white double flowers. They will tolerate most soils, but it must be moisture retentive and the plant must not be allowed to dry out. Site in full sun for the best show of flowers, although they will tolerate light shade.

Common name Deutzia.
Height 3m (10ft).
Colour White double flowers.
Flowering time Spring, summer.
Hardiness Hardy.
Leaves Deciduous.

3 m | PERIOD 1-2

ESCALLONIA 'SLIEVE DONARD' ESCALLONIA

A fast-growing shrub, suitable for the smaller garden. The flowers are bell-shaped and appear in late spring. Able to take most soils, except the most alkaline, they make very good wind-breaks near the sea.

Common name Escallonia.
Height 3m (10ft).
Colour White flowers.
Flowering time Spring.
Hardiness Hardy.
Leaves Evergreen.

3 m | PERIOD 1

EUPHORBIA PULCHERRIMA RED POINSETTIA

The most famous of the shrubby spurges. It is widely grown outside in hotter climates and used as a house plant in colder ones. It is characterised by the brilliant red bracts that surround the yellow flowers in winter.

Common name Poinsettia.
Height 1m (3ft).
Colour Brilliant red bracts, yellow flowers.
Flowering time Winter.
Hardiness Tender.
Leaves Deciduous.

 1 m PERIOD 4

FORSYTHIA X INTERMEDIA FORSYTHIA

One of three forms of *F.x intermedia* which has golden yellow flowers. The flowers are shaped like flared bells and appear before or just as the leaves are appearing in the early spring. It will grow almost anywhere, in full sun to flower at its best.

Common name Forsythia.
Height 4m (13ft).
Colour Golden yellow flowers.
Flowering time Spring.
Hardiness Hardy.
Leaves Deciduous.

 4 m PERIOD 1

FUCHSIA MAGELLANICA FUCHSIA

A popular species, with several well-known forms. It is the hardiest of the fuchsias. The flowers are small but free-flowering with a red top and purple lower half. Although they prefer sun, they can tolerate light shade.

Common name Fuchsia.
Height 1m (3ft).
Colour Red and purple.
Flowering time Summer, autumn.
Hardiness Hardy.
Leaves Deciduous.

FUCHSIA 'MRS POPPLE' FUCHSIA

This is one of the largest of the hardy varieties. It is an old and popular cultivar with a scarlet top and rich purple-violet skirt.

Common name Fuchsia.
Height 1m (3ft).
Colour Scarlet and purple.
Flowering time Summer, autumn.
Hardiness Hardy.
Leaves Deciduous.

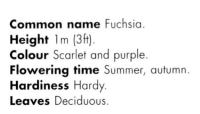

F
U
C
H
S
I
A

GARRYA ELLIPTICA TASSEL BUSH

A winter flowering shrub, with chains of grey-green flowers hanging among glossy green leaves. It can be sited on a north wall or grown as a free-standing shrub. The soil can be alkaline or acid, the position either in sun or partial shade.

Common name Tassel Bush.
Height 4m (13ft).
Colour Grey-green flowers.
Flowering time Winter.
Hardiness Hardy.
Leaves Evergreen.

4 m

PERIOD 4

HAMAMELIS MOLLIS CHINESE WITCH HAZEL

Considered to be one of the finest of all the winter-flowering shrubs. It bears knots of thin yellow ribbons, ties around naked branches. The centre of the petals has a red glow. Good for cutting and bringing indoors. Prefers neutral soils and full sun, but will tolerate light shade.

Common name Chinese Witch Hazel.
Height 5m (16ft).
Colour Yellow scented flowers.
Flowering time Winter.
Hardiness Hardy.
Leaves Deciduous.

5 m

PERIOD 4

HEBE SALICIFOLIA SHRUBBY VERONICA

This is a quick-growing shrub with long, pale mauve flower spikes that are strongly scented. The flowering season is long from early summer to late autumn. Site in full sun in free draining soil of any type. Salt tolerant they are an ideal seaside garden plant.

Common name Shrubby Veronica.
Height 2m (6ft).
Colour Pale mauve scented flowers.
Flowering time Summer, autumn.
Hardiness Hardy.
Leaves Evergreen.

HEBE 'MIDSUMMER BEAUTY' SHRUBBY VERONICA

This is a shrub with very long, scented lavender-purple flower spikes that are scented. Very decorative plants with long leaves, they can be grown in pots if winter protection is provided. The flowering season is long from early summer to late autumn.

Common name Shrubby Veronica.
Height 2m (6ft).
Colour Lavender-purple flowers.
Flowering time Summer, autumn.
Hardiness Hardy.
Leaves Evergreen.

H
E
B
E

HELIANTHEMUM NUMMULARIUM ROCK ROSE

A versatile plant which can be used in a wide variety of positions. The flowers are small, lasting only a day, but continuous bud renewal ensures a permanent display of flowers. They make good filler plants in herbaceous borders as their girth is two to three times greater than their height.

Common name Rock Rose.
Height 30cm (1ft).
Colour Primrose yellow flowers.
Flowering time Summer, autumn.
Hardiness Hardy.
Leaves Deciduous.

 30 cm **PERIOD 2-3**

HIBISCUS ROSA-SINENSIS ROSE OF SHARON

A member of the Mallow family, this is a tender plant suitable for growing outside in a warm, frost-free area. It makes an excellent shrub for the conservatory or greenhouse. If grown in a tub it can be moved to a sunny patio in the summer.

Common name Rose of Sharon.
Height 2m (6ft).
Colour Red flowers.
Flowering time Late summer.
Hardiness Tender.
Leaves Deciduous.

 2 m **PERIOD 2**

HYDRANGEA MACROPHYLLA HYDRANGEA

This has both mop-head and lacecap
cultivars in its ranks. The colours of the
flowers are influenced by the type of soil
they are planted in. Alkaline soil tends
to produce pink flowers; moved to acid
soil they will turn blue. They are hungry
plants preferring rich soil, regular
feeding and light shade for optimum
flowering.

Common name Hydrangea.
Height 2m (6ft).
Colour Pink to blue flowers.
Flowering time Summer, autumn.
Hardiness Hardy.
Leaves Deciduous.

HYDRANGEA INVOLUCRATA 'HORTENSIS' HYDRANGEA

A small delicate shrub whose double
lacecap flowers have a reddish tinge to
lilac or rose colouring, with white florets
round the outside. As above, the soil
type will affect the final colour of the
flowers.

Common name Hydrangea.
Height 1m (3ft).
Colour Pink to blue flowers.
Flowering time Summer, autumn.
Hardiness Hardy.
Leaves Deciduous.

H
Y
D
R
A
N
G
E
A

HYDRANGEA SARGENTIANA HYDRANGEA

A large shrub with large, furry leaves up to 25cm (10in) which needs space in a garden. They colour well in autumn. The flowers have pink or blue centres and white outer flowers.

Common name Hydrangea.
Height 3m (10ft).
Colour Pink to blue flowers.
Flowering time Summer, autumn.
Hardiness Hardy.
Leaves Deciduous.

3 m

PERIOD 2-3

HYPERICUM HIDCOTE ST JOHN'S WORT

One of the most popular hypericums as it is constantly covered in yellow flowers. If it gets leggy, it can be cut back all over by a third in spring. This is able to withstand severe frosts, shooting again from the base.

Common name St John's Wort.
Height 2m (6ft).
Colour Golden yellow flowers.
Flowering time Summer, autumn.
Hardiness Hardy.
Leaves Deciduous.

2 m

PERIOD 2-3

JASMINUM NUDIFLORUM WINTER JASMINE

A popular jasmine as it flowers in winter with masses of golden yellow flowers when nothing much else in the garden is flowering. It can be trained well against a wall, even a north wall.

Common name Winter Jasmine.
Height 1m (3ft).
Colour Yellow flowers.
Flowering time Summer, autumn, winter.
Hardiness Hardy.
Leaves Evergreen.

1 m | PERIOD 2-4

JASMINUM OFFICINALE COMMON JASMINE

Popular due to its fragrant flowers, Common Jasmine carries white flowers. It is a rampant climber. There is also a variegated version.

Common name Common jasmine.
Height 1m (3ft).
Colour White scented flowers.
Flowering time Late summer, autumn.
Hardiness Hardy.
Leaves Evergreen.

1 m | PERIOD 2-3

J A S M I N U M

KALMIA LATIFOLIA MOUNTAIN LAUREL

This plant is related to the rhododendron. The stamens have brown anthers, giving a speckled look to the flowers. The leaves are leathery and elliptic. These plants dislike alkaline soils and need soil similar to that preferred by rhododendrons.

Common name Mountain Laurel.
Height 3m (10ft).
Colour Pink flowers.
Flowering time Summer.
Hardiness Hardy.
Leaves Evergreen.

 3 m **PERIOD 2**

KERRIA JAPONICA JEW'S MALLOW

A slender shrub with cane-like stems with single flowers. A perfectly hardy, tolerating most soils, and is happy in either sun or light shade, flowering better in the former. It should be planted beside other shrubs, as it suckers too freely to be happy in a herbaceous border.

Common name Jew's Mallow.
Height 2m (6ft).
Colour Yellow flowers.
Flowering time Spring.
Hardiness Hardy.
Leaves Deciduous.

 2 m **PERIOD 1**

LAVANDULA ANGUSTIFOLIA OLD ENGLISH LAVENDER

A nostalgic plant reminiscent of cottage gardens, with a smell that no-one forgets. This can be found confusingly under other names in garden centres namely: *L.officinalis*, *L.spica* and *L. spicata*. This plant can be used both formally or informally in free-draining soil of any type.

Common name Old English Lavender.
Height 45cm (18in).
Colour Lavender blue flowers.
Flowering time Summer, autumn.
Hardiness Hardy.
Leaves Evergreen.

 45 cm **PERIOD 2-3**

LAVATERA OLBIA TREE MALLOW

This is the more refined of the mallows and has pink flowers, with darker veining. It is mainly known in its form 'Rosea', which is widely available. It will flower throughout the summer and autumn. Propagation is from cuttings.

Common name Tree Mallow.
Height 3m (10ft).
Colour Pink flowers.
Flowering time Summer.
Hardiness Semi-hardy.
Leaves Deciduous.

 3 m **PERIOD 2**

LAVANDULA/LAVATERA

LEPTOSPERMUM SCOPARIUM 'RED DAMASK' TEA TREE

This plant has fragrant leaves when crushed, and can be tender so they are best planted in tubs so they can be given winter protection. The flowers are small in the form of discs with a darker centre. The leaves are small and can be brewed to make a sort of tea, hence the vernacular name.

Common name Tea Tree.
Height 5m (16ft).
Colour Pink flowers.
Flowering time Summer, autumn.
Hardiness Tender.
Leaves Evergreen.

5 m | PERIOD 2-3 | |

LEPTOSPERMUM LANIGERUM TEA TREE

These plants should be provided with light, free-draining soils in full sun. They prefer sheltered positions and are ideal against a wall near paths, where they can be appreciated close to. This plant is considered to be hardier than the more common *L. scoparium*.

Common name Tea Tree.
Height 5m (16ft).
Colour Pure white flowers.
Flowering time Summer, autumn.
Hardiness Hardy.
Leaves Evergreen.

5 m | PERIOD 2-3 | |

LEYCESTERIA FORMOSA HIMALAYAN HONEYSUCKLE

A plant often planted on pheasant shoot areas as these birds love the gooseberry-like berries. The stems are hollow, similar to canes, and are bright green. It regenerates freely and quickly from seed, so any loss is quickly replaced.

Common name Himalayan Honeysuckle, Elisha's Tears.
Height 3m (10ft).
Colour Crimson bracts and white flowers.
Flowering time Summer, autumn.
Hardiness Hardy.
Leaves Evergreen.

 3 m PERIOD 2-3

LIGUSTRUM VULGARE EUROPEAN PRIVET

Although a common hedging specimen, there are at least 20 different varieties of privet any of which can make a fine specimen plant. If left to grow freely it can produce masses of white flowers. There are several forms, including golden ones.

Common name European Privet.
Height 6m (20ft).
Colour White flowers.
Flowering time Summer.
Hardiness Hardy.
Leaves Evergreen.

 6 m PERIOD 2

LONICERA TRAGOPHYLLA HONEYSUCKLE

Although this is one of the showiest species with large, bright yellow flowers, it is not scented. They will grow almost anywhere, in most soils but will flower better in full sun. An ideal climber for a wall or archway.

Common name Honeysuckle.
Height 3m (10ft).
Colour Yellow flowers.
Flowering time Summer.
Hardiness Hardy.
Leaves Deciduous.

3
m

PERIOD
2

LONICERA PERICLYMENUM 'BELGICA' DUTCH HONEYSUCKLE

This is also known as Early Dutch Honeysuckle which has been grown for many years due to its fragrance. The flowers are purple-red, fading to a pink yellow.

Common name Dutch Honeysuckle.
Height 3m (10ft).
Colour Purple-red flowers.
Flowering time Summer.
Hardiness Hardy.
Leaves Deciduous.

3
m

PERIOD
2

MAGNOLIA STELLATA STAR MAGNOLIA

This is a small shrub commonly seen in small gardens. The spring flowers are white and appear before the leaves and continue for quite a long time. A true specimen plant that should not be placed in a herbaceous border as the roots resent disturbance.

Common name Star Magnolia.
Height 3m (10ft).
Colour White flowers.
Flowering time Spring.
Hardiness Hardy.
Leaves Deciduous.

 3 m PERIOD **1**

MAGNOLIA x SOULANGIANA MAGNOLIA

This shrub has big, upright goblet flowers of white, or pale pink slightly stained with purple. This shrub can grow to10m (30ft) and has many varieties.

Common name Magnolia.
Height 10m (30ft).
Colour White of pale pink flowers.
Flowering time Spring.
Hardiness Hardy.
Leaves Deciduous.

 10 m PERIOD **1**

MAHONIA JAPONICA OREGON GRAPE

This plant flowers from late autumn to late spring. The flowers are followed by black or purple berries. They are able to take full sun or partial shade in any type of soil. A useful plant for livening up the garden in winter and the glossy foliage can be used to accent other plants later in the season.

Common name Oregon Grape.
Height 2m (6ft).
Colour Sulphur yellow flowers.
Flowering time Autumn to spring.
Hardiness Hardy.
Leaves Evergreen.

 2 m PERIOD 3-1

NERIUM OLEANDER OLEANDER

A splendid long-flowering shrub for frost-free areas. They prefer well-drained soil in full sun to produce tubular, fragrant flowers which can be single or double. Good container plants for the conservatory where they can be moved outside in summer.

Common name Oleander.
Height 4m (13ft).
Colour White, pink, red to pale yellow flowers.
Flowering time Summer.
Hardiness Hardy.
Leaves Evergreen.

 4 m PERIOD 2

OLEARIA HAASTIIS DAISY BUSH

When in flower, this plant is covered in daisy-like flowers, with the typical yellow central disc and ray-like petals. Out of season it is a drab plant. They are salt tolerant, so are a good seaside plant. This is the commonest form available and is reasonably hardy.

Common name Daisy Bush.
Height 3m (10ft).
Colour White flowers.
Flowering time Summer, autumn.
Hardiness Semi-hardy.
Leaves Evergreen.

 3 m **PERIOD 2-3**

OSMANTHUS x BURKWOODII OSMANTHUS

A good specimen to add to the back of a shrub border or to make a thick hedge. The flowers are small, but appear in great numbers with a fragrant scent. The leaves are ovate and glossy. The plants are happiest in full sun, but will take light shade, and benefit from a trim after flowering.

Common name Osmanthus.
Height 4m (13ft).
Colour White flowers.
Flowering time Spring.
Hardiness Hardy.
Leaves Evergreen.

 4 m **PERIOD 1**

OZOTHAMNUS ROSMARINIFOLIUM HELICHRYSUM

Needle-like leaves adorn this plant from Australia and they are attractive all-year round. The flowers are very small but in tight flat-head bunches, so they show up well against the green foliage. Similar in shape and colour to rosemary, from which it gets its name.

Common name Helichrysum.
Height 1m (3ft).
Colour Pinkish white flowers.
Flowering time Spring.
Hardiness Hardy.
Leaves Evergreen.

 1 m PERIOD 1

PAEONIA SUFFRUCTICOSA 'ROCK'S VARIETY' MOUTAN

An attractive plant for the back of the border or as a specimen plant in a tub. Their main disadvantage is the short flowering season. The flowers are huge, white and with blotches at the base.

Common name Moutan.
Height 2m (6ft).
Colour White flowers.
Flowering time Summer.
Hardiness Hardy.
Leaves Deciduous.

 2 m PERIOD 2

PAEONIA DELAVAYI TREE PEONY

This shrub has very deep, rich red
flowers and a boss of golden anthers.
Slightly shorter in stature than others, it
tends to sucker, though not to the extent
that this becomes a nuisance.

Common name Tree Peony.
Height 2m (6ft).
Colour Deep red flowers.
Flowering time Summer.
Hardiness Hardy.
Leaves Deciduous.

 2 m PERIOD 2

PEROVSKIA ATRIPLICIFOLIA RUSSIAN SAGE

This is a small airy shrub, with each
branch end covered in a spray of small
lavender-blue flowers. The leaves are a
soft grey and it is a good plant to
include in a mixed border. They will
take a range of soils so long as they are
well-drained. Each year, it is cut to the
ground.

Common name Russian Sage.
Height 1m (3ft).
Colour Blue flowers.
Flowering time Summer, autumn.
Hardiness Hardy.
Leaves Deciduous.

 1 m PERIOD 2-3

PHILADELPHUS 'BELLE ETOILE' MOCK ORANGE

An excellent form of this genus with fragrant single flowers with a dark pink centre. The leaves are medium-sized, ovate leaves which set off the white flowers to good effect. They will thrive in most soils so long as they are fertile. Equally happy in sun or light shade.

Common name Mock Orange.
Height 2m (6ft).
Colour White flowers with dark pink centres.
Flowering time Summer.
Hardiness Hardy.
Leaves Deciduous.

 2 m **PERIOD 2**

PHILADELPHUS 'SYBILLE' MOCK ORANGE

A small variety of this genus with very large white flowers with rose pink towards the base. The leaves provide a good contrast to the white flowers. They make good specimen plants or can be planted in groups. They are useful in a herbaceous border.

Common name Mock Orange.
Height 1m (3ft).
Colour White flowers.
Flowering time Summer.
Hardiness Hardy.
Leaves Deciduous.

 1 m **PERIOD 2**

PHLOMIS FRUCTICOSA JERUSALEM SAGE

A loose shrub that prefers full sun. The leaves are heavily-felted and whorls of sage-like flowers stack up the stems. The leaves are grey-green and along with the stems are clothed in fine hairs. Soil needs to free-draining.

Common name Jerusalem Sage.
Height 1m (3ft).
Colour Yellow flowers.
Flowering time Summer.
Hardiness Hardy.
Leaves Evergreen.

PHOTINIA x FRASERI 'RED ROBIN' PHOTINIA

An evergreen shrub grown for its brilliant red young leaves which appear in spring. It is a good plant for an evergreen hedge as its growth is vigorous. Best planted in sun in ordinary, well-drained soil.

Common name Photinia.
Height 2m (6ft).
Colour White flowers.
Flowering time Late spring, early Summer.
Hardiness Hardy.
Leaves Evergreen.

PIERIS FORMOSA FORRESTII 'WAKEHURST' ANDROMEDA

This is one of the best known species. The leaves and flowers are equally attractive. The flowers hang from the branches in spring, followed by fiery-red growth of new leaves. They dislike chalky soils and prefer a light shady position where they will not receive early morning sun in spring.

Common name Andromeda.
Height 4m (13ft).
Colour White flowers.
Flowering time Summer.
Hardiness Hardy.
Leaves Deciduous.

4 m

PERIOD **2**

PITTOSPORUM TENUFOLIUM 'SILVER QUEEN' PITTOSPORUM

A slow growing shrub which can make an excellent hedging plant. The silvery leaves are edged in white. They like well-drained soil, positioned out of the wind. The flowers are fragrant white and popular for flower arranging.

Common name Pittosporum.
Height 3m (10ft).
Colour White flowers.
Flowering time Late spring to early summer.
Hardiness Hardy.
Leaves Evergreen.

3 m

PERIOD **1-2**

POTENTILLA DAVURICA 'ABBOTSWOOD' CINQUEFOIL

This plant forms a compact bush with white, flat saucer-shaped flowers, with five petals which flower over a long period. The leaves are small, made up of five or three leaflets. Although deciduous, new growth appears early in the year. Best in full sun but will tolerate a little shade.

Common name Cinquefoil.
Height 1m (3ft).
Colour White flowers.
Flowering time Summer.
Hardiness Hardy.
Leaves Deciduous.

 1 m PERIOD 2

POTENTILLA PARVIFLORA CINQUEFOIL

This is a small shrub with small leaves, each composed of seven leaflets. The flowers are also on the small side and are a rich yellow colour. Happy in most soils but prefers full sun. Popular plants as they are compact and very useful in any border as they blend with a range of colours.

Common name Cinquefoil.
Height 1m (3ft).
Colour Yellow flowers.
Flowering time Summer.
Hardiness Hardy.
Leaves Deciduous.

 1 m PERIOD 2

PRUNUS TENELLA 'FIRE HILL' FLOWERING ALMOND

A shrubby cherry with upright branches clothed in dark rose-pink flowers, just as the leaves are breaking. The flowers hang in clusters in early spring, covering the tree. Although totally hardy, although damage to blossom can be occur due to late frosts.

Common name Flowering Almond.
Height 1m (3ft).
Colour Dark rose-pink flowers.
Flowering time Spring.
Hardiness Hardy.
Leaves Deciduous.

RHODODENDRON LUTEUM AZALEA

The commonest and easiest to grow of all the azaleas. The fat flower buds appear on the shrub the moment the leaves fall in October, remaining all winter before bursting into bloom in May.

Common name Azalea.
Height 2.4m (8ft).
Colour Yellow flowers.
Flowering time Spring.
Hardiness Hardy.
Leaves Deciduous.

RHODODENDRON PONTICUM RHODODENDRON

This is sometimes used as an informal screen or large hedge to provide wind protection. Native to Portugal and Spain, it is now naturalised in many parts of the world. The plant should be pruned after flowering.

Common name Rhododendron.
Height 2m (6ft).
Colour Mauve flowers.
Flowering time Spring.
Hardiness Hardy.
Leaves Deciduous.

RHODODENDRON YAKUSHIMANUM RHODODENDRON

A striking evergreen shrub, popular as a parent to a number of hybrids due to its compactness and its hardiness. The leaves are fairly long and bear pale buff felt on the undersides.

Common name Rhododendron.
Height 60cm (2ft).
Colour Pink flowers fading to white.
Flowering time Spring.
Hardiness Hardy.
Leaves Evergreen.

RHODODENDRON

RIBES SANGUINEUM FLOWERING CURRANT

One of the earliest shrubs to burst into leaf and flower. The flowers appear as tassles on this hardy shrub. Most soils are acceptable, in full sun or light shade. Best placed at the back of the border as once flowering is finished there is not much to look at for the rest of the season.

Common name Flowering Currant.
Height 2.1m (7ft).
Colour Pink flowers.
Flowering time Spring.
Hardiness Hardy.
Leaves Deciduous.

 2.1 m PERIOD 1

ROBINIA HISPIDA ROSE ACACIA

A member of the pea family, the flowers hang in long trusses in summer. Light green, pinnate leaves ensure this shrub looks fresh and light. Tolerant of air pollution, making them ideal for planting in town gardens. They do need shelter from strong winds and prefer full sun. Thorns cover the branches.

Common name Rose Acacia.
Height 2.4m (8ft).
Colour Rose-pink flowers.
Flowering time Summer.
Hardiness Hardy.
Leaves Deciduous.

 2.4 m PERIOD 2

ROMNEYA COULTERI TREE POPPY

This is a very attractive Californian shrub. The flowers are up to 15cm (6in) across and sweetly fragrant. They continue to appear throughout the summer, well into the autumn. The leaves are a blue-green. The shrub mildly suckers making a dense clump.

Common name Tree Poppy.
Height 2m (6ft).
Colour White flowers with large golden stamens.
Flowering time Summer, autumn.
Hardiness Hardy.
Leaves Deciduous.

 2 m PERIOD 2-3

ROSA 'ENA HARKNESS' HYBRID TEA ROSE

A large-flowered rose which has been traditionally used in bedding and heavily pruned each year. Flowering continuously over the summer, the plants are rather formal with a single crimson bloom per stem. They prefer fertile soil, enriched with manure.

Common name Hybrid Tea Rose.
Height 1.2m (4ft).
Colour Crimson flowers.
Flowering time Summer, autumn.
Hardiness Hardy.
Leaves Deciduous.

 1.2 m PERIOD 2-3

ROSA 'PINK PARFAIT' FLORIBUNDA ROSE

A traditional bedding plant, similar to hybrid teas, but having several blooms per stem. Plant in full sun to get the best out of these roses. The soil should be enriched with manure.

Common name Floribunda Rose.
Height 1.2m (4ft).
Colour Pink flowers.
Flowering time Summer, autumn.
Hardiness Hardy.
Leaves Deciduous.

1.2 m

PERIOD 2-3

ROSA 'DOROTHY PERKINS' RAMBLER ROSE

These roses shoot upwards with very long, arching stems. They are ideal for covering sheds, banks, fences or pergolas. There is a single flower display each in a year with pink flowers. They need tying to supports.

Common name Rambler Rose.
Height 6m (18ft).
Colour Pink flowers.
Flowering time Summer, autumn.
Hardiness Hardy.
Leaves Deciduous.

6 m

PERIOD 2-3

ROSA

ROSA 'FRAU DAGMAR HASTRUP' SHRUB ROSE

This plant is grown in a more informal manner than the hybrid teas and floribundas. They are bred as free-ranging bushes suitable for use in a mixed border. They like rich, moist soil in full sun for maximum blooms.

Common name Shrub Rose.
Height 2m (6ft).
Colour Pink flowers.
Flowering time Summer, autumn.
Hardiness Hardy.
Leaves Deciduous.

2 m | PERIOD 2-3

ROSA 'ZÉPHIRINE DROUCHIN' CLIMBER ROSE

This rose has semi-double, cerise pink flowers, which can flower continuously throughout the summer. They can be used to cover pergolas, sheds, trellis, archways but will require tying to supports. Plant in a rich moist soil, with added manure.

Common name Climber Rose.
Height 2.5m (8ft).
Colour Cerise pink flowers.
Flowering time Summer, autumn.
Hardiness Hardy.
Leaves Deciduous.

2.5 m | PERIOD 2-3

ROSMARINUS OFFICINALIS ROSEMARY

A much valued herb which has been in cultivation for many centuries. An attractive bush with violet-blue flowers, set against narrow linear leaves of grey green. It is fragrant and fairly hardy, but appreciates some protection from cold winds.

Common name Rosemary.
Height 2m (6ft).
Colour Violet-blue flowers.
Flowering time Summer.
Hardiness Hardy.
Leaves Evergreen.

2 m | PERIOD 2

SANTOLINA CHAMAECYPARISSUS COTTON LAVENDER

A fairly small shrub, considered to be half-way between hardy perennials and shrubs. They will tolerate any kind of soil, but it must be free-draining in full sun. They are suitable for rock gardens or on a bank. The silver foliage is the main attraction as the flowers are insignificant.

Common name Cotton Lavender.
Height 60cm (2ft).
Colour Yellow flowers.
Flowering time Summer, autumn.
Hardiness Hardy.
Leaves Deciduous.

60 cm | PERIOD 2-3

SENECIO GREYI SHRUBBY RAGWORT

A silver foliage plant with daisy-like, yellow flowers. They require a sunny position to flower well. They come from New Zealand, so are not completely hardy in colder areas. They are wind and salt tolerant, making them useful seaside shrubs.

Common name Shrubby Ragwort.
Height 2m (6ft).
Colour Yellow flowers.
Flowering time Summer.
Hardiness Hardy.
Leaves Evergreen.

SKIMMIA JAPONICA SKIMMIA

The leaves of this shrub are pale, and curved, exuding an orange scent when crushed. The plant forms a shallow dome and is invaluable in the garden for its tolerance of shade and lime, and also for its hardiness. The flowers on female plants, are followed by red berries which may last until February.

Common name Skimmia.
Height 2m (6ft).
Colour White fragrant flowers.
Flowering time Spring.
Hardiness Hardy.
Leaves Evergreen.

SOLANUM CRISPUM CHILEAN POTATO TREE

A member of the potato, tomato and deadly nightshade family. They can be tender but will regenerate if cut back by winter frosts. They have potato-like flowers and thrive in any soil. Full sun is preferred. They can be grown up a trellis or against a wall.

Common name Chilean Potato Tree.
Height 6m (18ft).
Colour Blue flowers.
Flowering time Summer, autumn.
Hardiness Tender.
Leaves Deciduous.

 6 m PERIOD 2-3

SPIREA ARGUTA BRIDAL WREATH

This is a wonderful spring-flowering plant with many arching, twiggy branches covered in masses of delicate, white flowers. They are extremely hardy. Full sun is preferred in any type of soil.

Common name Bridal Wreath.
Height 2m (6ft).
Colour White flowers.
Flowering time Spring.
Hardiness Hardy.
Leaves Deciduous.

 2 m PERIOD 1

SYRINGA MICROPHYLLA LILAC

This is an elegant small lilac suitable for gardens too small to grow a large hybrid. This variety has the typical lilac fragrance. The flush of blooms can cause the twigs to bow gracefully. There can be a second flowering in the autumn.

Common name Lilac.
Height 1m (3ft).
Colour Rose lilac flowers.
Flowering time Spring.
Hardiness Hardy.
Leaves Deciduous.

1 m · PERIOD 1

SYRINGA VULGARIS COMMON LILAC

This is the wild form known as Common Lilac and its flowers are a lilac colour. The leaves are ovate and the fragrant flowers are small, tubular and four petalled, held in large spikes. The are generally very hardy and happy on most soils, including chalk. Full sun is preferred but some shade is tolerated.

Common name Common Lilac.
Height 6m (20ft).
Colour Mauves and purple flowers.
Flowering time Spring.
Hardiness Hardy.
Leaves Deciduous.

6 m · PERIOD 1

VIBURNUM x BODNANTENSE VIBURNUM

This is a wonderful plant with clusters of pink flowers from late autumn right through the winter. They are very fragrant. The shrub can be awkward looking but the flowers are marvellous. They grow well on most soils, including chalk. They are frost resistant.

Common name Viburnum.
Height 3m (9ft).
Colour Pink flowers.
Flowering time Autumn, winter.
Hardiness Hardy.
Leaves Deciduous.

3
m

PERIOD
3-4

VIBURNUM x BURKWOODII VIBURNUM

This shrub begins to flower just as other viburnums are finishing. The pink buds open to form a large cluster of white flowers, with an overpowering scent. Some flowers open in February, with the main display being in April. An easy shrub to grow with shining dark green leaves.

Common name Viburnum.
Height 3m (9ft).
Colour White flowers.
Flowering time Autumn, winter.
Hardiness Hardy.
Leaves Evergreen.

3
m

PERIOD
3-4

VINCA MAJOR GREATER PERIWINKLE

An excellent ground cover plant with a tendency to scramble through other plants. The arching stems roots very easily allowing it to travel quickly over the ground. Plant with care. There is a variegated form.

Common name Greater Periwinkle.
Height 60 cm (2ft).
Colour Blue flowers.
Flowering time Spring, early summer.
Hardiness Hardy.
Leaves Evergreen.

 60 cm PERIOD 1-2

VINCA MINOR LESSER PERIWINKLE

This is a smaller version of vinca major which spreads just as quickly. The stems, leaves and flowers are smaller but it blooms for a longer period, from March to July. Variegated forms exist.

Common name Lesser Periwinkle.
Height 30 cm (1ft).
Colour Purple or white flowers.
Flowering time Spring, summer.
Hardiness Hardy.
Leaves Evergreen.

 30 cm PERIOD 1-2

VINCA

WEIGELA FLORIDA 'VARIEGATA' WEIGELA

A popular plant for the garden which is at its height in late spring and early summer. The flowers appear as masses of flared funnels in pinks with green and yellow foliage. They grow on any soil in full sun, but will tolerate some shade.

Common name Weigela.
Height 2m (6ft).
Colour Pink flowers.
Flowering time Spring, early summer.
Hardiness Hardy.
Leaves Deciduous.

2 m | PERIOD 1-2

WISTERIA FLORIBUNDA 'MULTIJUGA' WISTERIA

This is not a plant for small gardens unless drastically pruned each year. The racemes on this variety can reach up to 1m (3ft) in length. They will tolerate most soils if it is well drained. They can be trained to grow over structures or even trees, in addition to clambering over the walls of a house.

Common name Wisteria.
Height 30m (70ft).
Colour Pale purple flowers.
Flowering time Spring.
Hardiness Hardy.
Leaves Deciduous.

30 m | PERIOD 1

Index Alphabetical listing of botanical names.

I N D E X

Index
Alphabetical listing of common names.

I N D E X